BIGMAMA

Harbor
Donald Crews

MULBERRY BOOKS · New York

Manufactured in China.

10 11 12 13 SCP 10

Library of Congress Cataloging in Publication Data

Crews, Donald. Harbor. Summary: Presents various kinds of boats which come and go in a busy harbor. 1. Ships—Pictorial works—Juvenile literature. [1. Harbors. 2. Boats] I. Title. VM307.C8   623.8'2'00222   81-66 ISBN 0-688-07332-8

First Mulberry Edition, 1987

the women in my life
Malcolm

A harbor.

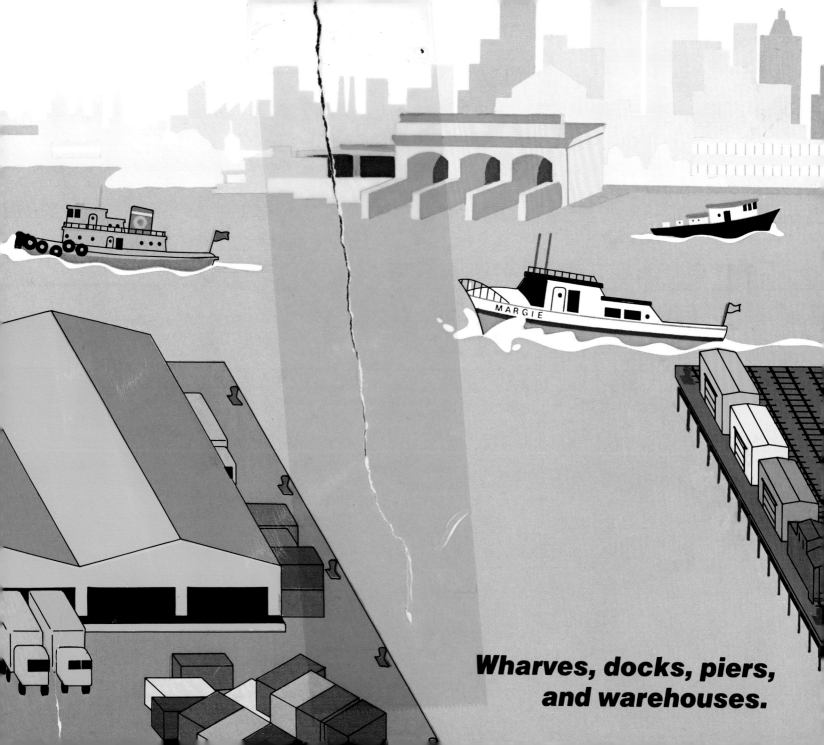

Wharves, docks, piers, and warehouses.

INDUSTRIAL CONSTRUCTION COR

ALICE

HARBOR PIER

A port for ships,
boats, and cargo.

Ferryboats shuttle back and forth from shore to shore. They do not need to turn around. The back becomes the front.

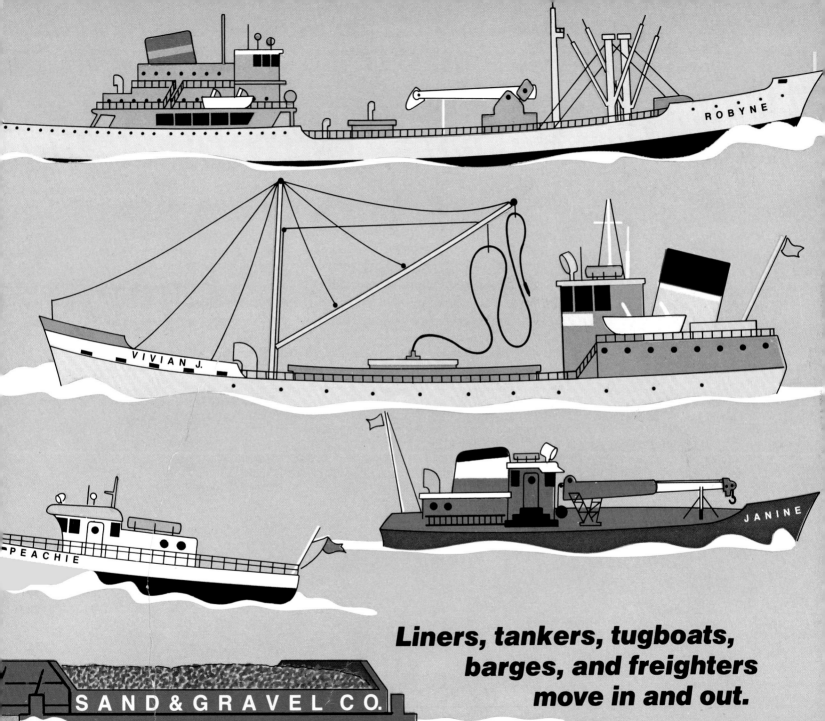

Liners, tankers, tugboats, barges, and freighters move in and out.

**Big boats,
little boats,**

long, low-lying barges,

fast police boats, and
slow-moving lighters
crowd the water.

The tugboat is the busiest boat in the harbor.

**Tugs push.
Tugs tow.**

*Tugs guide big boats
to their docks*

MALCOLM

AVA

and out again.

**In the harbor the fireboat
is ready for an emergency**

or a celebration.

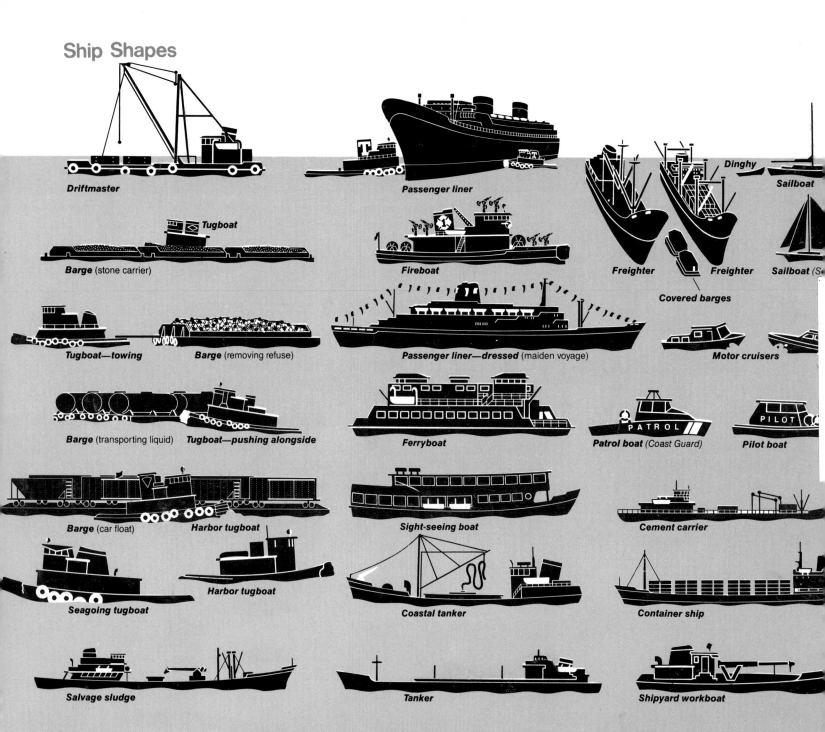

Ship Shapes

Driftmaster

Passenger liner

Dinghy

Sailboat

Tugboat

Barge (stone carrier)

Fireboat

Freighter   **Freighter**

Sailboat (S

Covered barges

Tugboat—towing   **Barge** (removing refuse)

Passenger liner—dressed (maiden voyage)

Motor cruisers

Barge (transporting liquid)   **Tugboat—pushing alongside**

Ferryboat

Patrol boat (Coast Guard)

Pilot boat

Barge (car float)   **Harbor tugboat**

Sight-seeing boat

Cement carrier

Seagoing tugboat

Harbor tugboat

Coastal tanker

Container ship

Salvage sludge

Tanker

Shipyard workboat